★ ★ ★

PHILADELPHIA
Phillies

JAMES R. ROTHAUS

CREATIVE EDUCATION

Library of Congress Cataloging-in-Publication Data

Rothaus, James.
  Philadelphia Phillies.
    10756
  Summary: A history of the baseball team that has been
playing in Philadelphia since 1883.
    1.Philadelphia Phillies (Baseball team) — History —
Juvenile literature. [1. Philadelphia Phillies (Baseball
team) — History.   2. Baseball — History]   I. Title.
GV875.P45R68   1987   796.357'64'0974811   87-22218
ISBN 0-88682-146-0

★ ★ ★
CONTENTS

COVER PHOTO
The one-and-only Mike Schmidt strikes a familiar pose after launching one of his towering homers in 1968.

PHOTO SPREAD (PAGE 2/3)
Steve Jeltz watches the throw come down on a steal attempt by Bob Dernier of the Chicago Cubs.

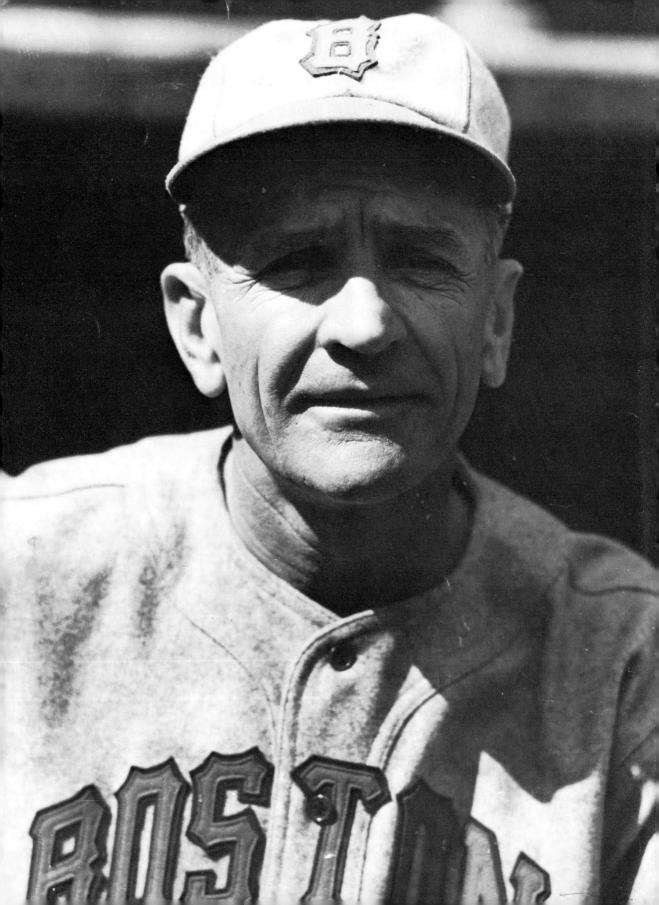

How old is the game of baseball in Philadelphia?

Very old. The first game in the history of the National League took place in the Quaker City in 1876. The Philadelphia Athletics took on Boston on April 22, at 25th and Jefferson Streets. Horse-drawn buggies surrounded the field. Baseball was a brand-new sport, and everyone turned out to watch.

Sadly, that first Philadelphia team broke up in mid-season. This left the fans without a National League club until 1883. That's when Alfred J. Reach traveled to Worcester, Mass., bought their local ball club and brought it to Philadelphia, adopting the team name "Phillies."

On May 1, more than 1,200 Philadelphia fans turned out to see their proud new Phillies meet the rugged Providence Grays at Recreation Park. That game was the start of a long tradition, rich with baseball legends and lore. Over the years, dozens of Philly players have been enshrined in Baseball's Hall of Fame. They include a Who's Who in American baseball—gallant men such as Ed Delahanty, Jimmie Foxx, Casey Stengel, Grover Alexander and Robin Roberts.

The Phillies' story is laced with fascinating ups and downs, highlighted by memorable World Championships in 1915, 1950 and 1980.

But first things first. Let's start with the most explosive Phillies team ever.

The Big Bats of 1894

No, they didn't win the World Series. In fact, these old-time Phillies finished fourth, behind Boston, Baltimore and league-leader New York.

May 1, 1883
The Philadelphia Phillies play their very first game (against the Providence Grays) at Recreation Park.

PHOTO
Casey Stengel, shown here in his Boston Manager's uniform in 1939, tabbed Phillie pitcher Grover Alexander as "The greatest N.L. pitcher ever."

The year was 1894.

Why was it a memorable team? Because these guys could *really* hit! In fact, their awesome batting statistics have never been equaled by any ball club in any era, past or present.

The leader was a guy named Ed Delahanty, who had hit .300 or better for 11 straight years. They called him the "Chief Executioner."

Consider the Phils' stats for 1894:
- 1,759 hits in 131 games
- an average of 13 hits a game
- a single-game record of 36 hits
- eight men with a combined batting average of .384.

In fact, this Philadelphia team had five men with a combined average of — would you believe? — .401! They included Turner, .523; Thompson, .403; Delahanty, .400; Hamilton, .398 and Lave Cross, .388. Power, pure and simple.

And finally Billy Hamilton, playing in 131 games that year, scored an unbeatable 196 runs for the Phillies, a feat no one has matched to date.

Babe Ruth got within sight of Hamilton's mark in 1921, but that's all. The Sultan of Swat, playing in 154 games, touched home plate 177 times.

The Phillies of 1894—a team for the all-time record books!

Alexander Leads Philly to First Pennant In 1915

When people talk about "the all-time pitchers in the history of baseball," you're bound to hear the names of Sandy Koufax, Cy Young, Lefty Grove, Bob Feller, Dizzy Dean, Herb Score, Walt Johnson, Warren Spahn,

Whitey Ford, and maybe a modern-day name or two, still trying to prove worthy of this company.

Most baseball experts, however, point to a select trio of pitchers as "the greatest." They are: Walter Johnson, winner of 414 games for the Washington Senators, the modern-era record, including 113 shutouts and 50 straight scoreless innings . . . Christy Mathewson, who in 16 years with the New York Giants posted 365 victories in a 14-year span, an average of 26 per year . . . and last, but not least, the Philadelphia Phillies' Grover Cleveland Alexander, who pitched 696 games, winning 373 (90 shutouts), including 266 strikeouts, and only 951 walks!

"I'd say that Alexander was the most amazing pitcher in the National League," said the legendary Casey Stengel, as he reviewed the past century. "Walter had to pitch in that little Philadelphia park with the big tin fence in right field. He pitched shutouts, which must mean he could do it. He had a fastball, a curve, a change-of-pace and perfect control. He was the best I batted against in the National League."

Just 24 when he signed on with the Phils in 1911, Alexander had his work cut out for him. The right-field fence in Baker Bowl ball park was only 250 feet from home plate, so he *had* to be a master strikeout artist.

It was Alexander who recorded 31 victories in the 1915 campaign to lead the Phillies to their first National League pennant. Give some credit to Phils' Manager Pat Moran, too. Moran was a genius at all angles of the game. His players even learned how to steal signs from opposing teams.

When the Phillies weren't on the field, Moran maintained strict discipline. No gambling or horseplay was allowed.

1916
The great
Grover Alexander
pitches 16 shutouts.

PHOTO
Hall-of-Famer
Grover Cleveland
Alexander remains
a Philadelphia
legend.

Spirits were high in the Quaker City. In the 1915 World Series opener against the confident Boston Red Sox, 19,343 fans were treated to another great pitching performance from Alexander, who beat the Sox, 3-1. It seemed the Phils were on their way to a World Series title, but Boston bounced back with three straight 2-1 victories, and a 5-4 clincher.

Once again, the World Championship had slipped through the mitts of a fine Philadelphia ball club, despite the best efforts of two future Hall-of-Famers— Grover Alexander and Dave Bancroft.

It would be 35 long years before another World Series would come to Philadelphia.

Robin Roberts Mows Down Dodgers for 1950 Title

Just when the fans had labeled them the "Fizz Kids," the Phillies came through like true Whiz Kids. On Oct. 2, 1950, they met the big, bad Brooklyn Dodgers at Ebbets Field for the National League Championship. The biggest Flatbush crowd of the season—35,073— turned out to watch Dodger ace Don Newcombe go against phenomenal Robin Roberts, of the Phillies. Roberts had already used his mystifying slider to win 19 games that season, but he figured the season would be a bust unless he could win No. 20 against the Dodgers that day. To do so, he would have to face the horrifying bats of Pee-Wee Reese, Duke Snider, Jackie Robinson and Gil Hodges!

After five innings, the Phillies held a slim, 1-0 lead. So far, so good. But Reese came to bat in the sixth, and hit a towering fly to right field. The ball lodged in a screen atop the wall. Pee-Wee waited on third, thinking the

PHOTO
Pitcher
Robin Roberts,
one of the 1950
"whiz kids" who
brought another
pennant to
Philadelphia.

ball had bounced in play. Finally the roar of the crowd convinced him he'd knotted the score.

The Dodgers threatened early in the 9th, but Phillies outfielder Richie Ashburn turned back a Dodgers go-ahead run with a rifle shot from center field to catcher Stan Lopata, cutting off Cal Abrams at the plate. Two away.

Like a Hollywood movie, the next batter was the one-and-only Gil Hodges, Brooklyn's leading home-run hitter. Hodges connected on a blast to center. The fans roared, sensing victory, but the ball fell into Del Ennis' glove. Three outs.

The 10th started with a Phillies rush. Pitcher Robin Roberts cracked a solid single up the middle. Waitkus dropped a pop-fly single into short center, out of everyone's reach. Ashburn put down a fine bunt.

Then Newcombe faced Dick Sisler, who had already hit three singles off the Dodger hurler. With the count 2 1, Sisler slapped the fourth pitch high into the sky toward left field. Abrams ran madly for the fence. No use. Only 348 feet from home plate, the fence couldn't stop young Sisler's biggest (and shortest) homer ever.

When Roberts faced the Dodgers in the 10th, it was one-two-three, taking out Roy Campanella, Jim Russell and Tommy Brown.

The N.L. pennant belonged to Philadelphia! Roberts had won No. 20 to become the first Philly hurler to win that many since the phenomenal Grover Cleveland Alexander turned in his third straight 30-game season in 1917.

Unfortunately, the Phillies would go against the New York Yankees in the 1950 World Series. The Yanks were

1934
For the first time,
the Phillies are
allowed to play
baseball on Sundays.

entering their dynasty era (1940-54), a period in which no mere mortals could bring them to defeat.

The Phillies fought gamely, losing 1-0, 2-1 (Roberts pitching 10 innings) in their home town, and then surrendered two more, 3-2 and 5-2, in Yankee Stadium. They did themselves proud, however, by limiting the Yanks to just two homers from "Joltin' Joe" DiMaggio and Yogi Berra in the four-game series.

In the years to come, pitcher Robin Roberts would go on to match Grover Alexander's record of six 20-win seasons. He closed out the 1952 campaign by notching his 28th victory of the year—a 7-4 decision over the New York Giants at the Polo Grounds. That superb effort made him the first National League pitcher to total that many wins since Dizzy Dean went 28-12 for the St. Louis Cardinals in 1935!

Jim Bunning Pitches Historic "Perfecto" In 1964

It was a sizzling-hot day in Shea Stadium on June 22, 1964, but Phillies pitcher Jim Bunning was even hotter. Bunning went out on the mound that day and recorded the National League's first perfect game in 84 years. A perfect game is one in which 27 batters come up—and go down—without anyone getting on base for the entire game!

PHOTO
Jim Bunning
strikes out
New York's
John Stephenson
for the final out
in a perfect
no-hit game. (1964)

Witnessed by 32,904 fans, the Bunning blitz was only the eighth perfect game in the 88-year history of major league baseball. Bunning's was the first in the majors since Don Larsen of the Yankees scuttled every Brooklyn Dodger that faced him in the fifth game of the 1956 World Series.

Even loyal Mets fans began rooting for Bunning in

the late innings at Shea Stadium. From the 7th on, the 32-year-old pitcher had everyone — except the Mets ballplayers — cheering for him. John Stephenson had the last shot at spoiling the day for Bunning, but the third strike came quickly, and No. 27 was retired.

The stands erupted with a booming cheer. Bunning was mobbed by his teammates, and returned to the field for a well-deserved bow as the fans chanted, "We want Bunning! We want Bunning!" It was one of the biggest ovations ever heard at Shea Stadium, drowning out sportcaster Ralph Kiner's post-game TV interview.

Before Bunning, the N.L. hadn't seen such mound mastery since John M. Ward tossed a "perfecto" for Providence against Buffalo on June 17, 1880. In those days, of course, the old-time pitchers had some unusual rules in their favor. The distance from the mound to home was only 45 feet, instead of the modern 60 feet, 6 inches. A pitcher could waste nine balls before the ump would walk a batter and, best of all, any foul ball caught on the first bounce was an out!

Jim Bunning did it the hard way. Using his fluid, three-quarter motion, he took out 10 Mets on strikes.

Excellent fielding from his Phillies teammates snuffed out the rest.

The Mets' Jessie Gonder came closest to spoiling Bunning's day. In the fifth, he hit a shot halfway between second baseman Tony Taylor and first baseman John Herrnstein. Taylor made a diving stab for the ball, stretching himself horizontally above the ground. The ball was so hard-hit that when it reached Taylor's glove, Gonder had only managed a third of the way to first. Taylor's quickness got the ball to Herrnstein for the out, saving the perfect game for Bunning — and history.

July 4, 1938
After playing 51 seasons at Baker Bowl, the Phillies move to Shibe Park. They split a double-header with Boston that day.

PHOTO
Infielder
Don Demeter anchors the Phillies infield against the Braves in '63.

May 16, 1939
Philadelphia plays its
very first night game
under the lights.

1980 Brings A World Championship!

The 1980 campaign would be a glorious one for the Philadelphia Phillies.

Now, after 97 years of National League play, the Phillies entered their third duel for the Championship of the World. The aging players rallied 'round three extraordinary athletes: Mike Schmidt, the easy front-runner for MVP honors with 44 homers, 114 RBIs and a .281 average; Steve Carlton, who would win the year's Cy Young Award with his 23-9 record; and Tug McGraw, the ace reliever who rose up from the sick bed just in time to slam the door for 11 saves.

After steamrolling the Houston Astros to win the National League Pennant, the Phillies took on Kansas City and their superstar George Brett in the best-of-seven World Series.

Believe it or not, in Game No. 1, the Phils started a 23-year-old rookie, Bob "Whirly-bird" Walk, against a 20-game winner—Dennis Leonard of Kansas City. The last time a rookie was so honored was back in 1952 When Dodger Joe Black had taken on the Yankees.

By the third inning, Walk had surrendered two-run homers to Amos Otis and Willie Aikens, giving the Royals a comfortable lead.

Larry Bowa started a Phillies rally in the bottom of the third, ending in Bake McBride's three-run shot to right field. The Phils added two more runs in the fourth and fifth to make it 7-4, Philadelphia.

Aikens of the Royals slapped his second two-run homer off Walk in the eighth. That was good-bye for the rookie, and Tug McGraw was asked to pitch his

PHOTO
Tug McGraw,
the pitcher who
never grew old,
uncorks a screwball
in the 1980
World Series.

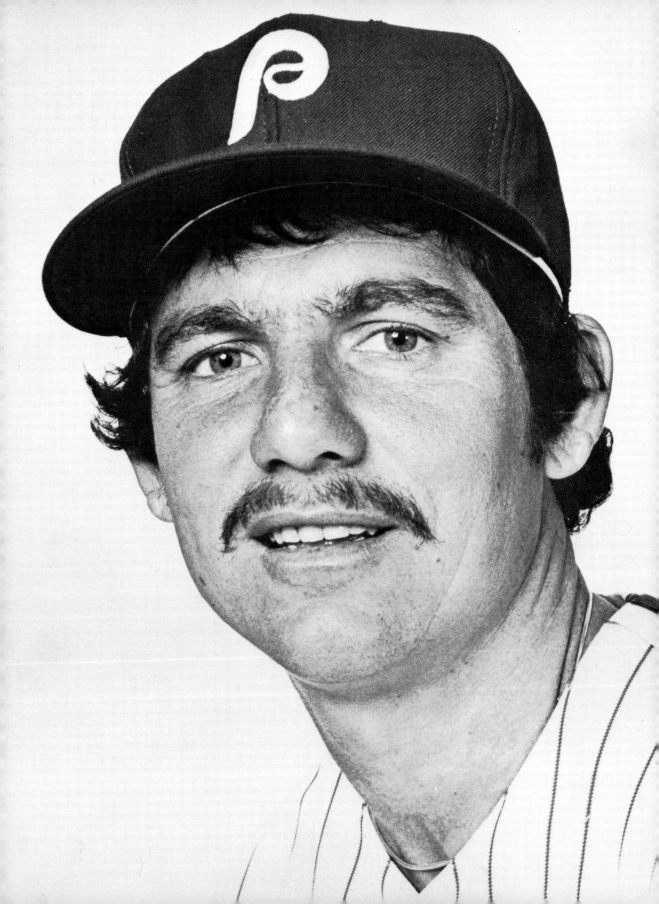

fifth straight post-season relief. Using his screwball, Tug put a lock on the K.C. batters. Final, 7-6, Phillies.

During a post-game talk with reporters, McGraw was asked if his pitching was mostly mental. "If that were true," he laughed, "I'd be in the trainers' room right now, soaking my head in ice."

In Game No. 2, the Royals' Amos Otis came through with a bases-loaded single past Mike Schmidt that gave K.C. the lead, 3-2, in the seventh.

Royals sinkerball specialist Dan Quisenberry (33 saves, 12 wins) relieved starter Larry Gura, and was easily snuffing out Phils until the eighth. That's when 35-year-old Del Unser, a 13-year veteran, began a Philly rally. His double scored Bob Boone from first; Pete Rose advanced Del, who then scored on McBride's hit. Schmidt doubled in McBride, and Keith Moreland came through as a designated hitter, scoring Schmidt. Final 6-4, Phillies.

Game No. 3 went back to Kansas City where the Royals took a 4-3 squeaker, primarily because the frustrated Phils left a total of 15 runners stranded on base.

Game No. 4 belonged to K.C.'s Willy Mays Aikens. The big man swatted two homers (making a total of four for the series), which tied the records of legendary players Snider, Gehrig and Ruth.

Aikens' first homer in Game 4 sailed all the way into the Royals' waterfall in right center, scoring Brett. His second finally came to earth in the Royals' bullpen in right. The Royals won, 5-3, to even the Series.

In Game No. 5, everyone was beginning to wonder if Philly had run out of miracles. The situation looked bleak with K.C. leading by a run in the 7th, but the "Come-From-Behind Kids" wouldn't be denied. Working against ace Quisenberry, second baseman Manny

March 8, 1941
The first player to enter military service for World War II is Philadelphia's Hugh N. Mulcahy.

PHOTO
Larry Bowa was the man who could rally the Phillies when the chips were down.

Trillo poked a sinker right back at the pitcher.

"The ball hit my glove, then the tips of the fingers of my right hand," recalled Quisenberry. "I didn't have time to think. I saw it at the last second, then I played hide and seek with it." The result was an RBI, scoring Unser— the Phils' fourth and go-ahead run.

McGraw didn't make it easy for himself in the ninth. Nursing a one-run lead, Tug loaded the bases. K.C.'s Jose Cardenal, a great clutch-hitter, was the next batter. After McGraw worked the count to 1-2, he called time. The Kansas City organ player struck up a lively polka. McGraw and Boone met to plan strategy while the crowd roared support for the nervous Cuban batter.

McGraw was ready. Cardenal was ready. The fastball whistled into Boone's glove. Cardenal had taken his best cut. Strike three. Now the Phils were just one victory away from the crown.

Game No. 6 turned into a real nail-biter in the final innings. Carlton pitched a beautiful game, giving the Phils a 4-1 lead in the seventh. It was up to McGraw to protect that lead over the final two innings. With two outs in the ninth, however, Tug had once again loaded the bases. Up strode Willie Wilson, representing the possible winning run for Kansas City.

McGraw remembers it this way: "I look for a way to muster up some gusto in crises such as this one." Noticing some German shepherds moving along the sidelines with the police, Tug thought, "What I am is dog tired, and I could really use a 'K' (the symbol for a strikeout) right now. This is no time to dog it!"

Tug McGraw, his arm and hand going numb from nine appearances in 11 post-season games, was now

1954
Philadelphia slugger Vince DiMaggio crunches four grand-slam home runs— a club record that still stands.

PHOTO AT LEFT
Bake McBride follows the flight of his three-run homer in the 1980 World Series.

PHOTO SPREAD NEXT PAGE
Two of baseball's all-time greats— Steve Garvey and Mike Schmidt— caught on camera in 1982 action at Dodger Stadium.

mentally ready for Willie Wilson. A screwball was a called strike. "I wanted to show Wilson I wasn't afraid to throw a breaking ball," said McGraw. Next came a hard slider, breaking in on Wison's bat; he fouled it off for strike two. A fastball got away, going high for ball one. Count: 1-2.

Catcher Bob Boone flashed McGraw a series of signs, which the pitcher shook off. Then McGraw came with his patented fastball, slightly up on the inside of the plate. Wilson took a cut, missed, and 65,838 Philadelphians filled the night air with shouts of relief and celebration. The Philadelphia Phillies were 1980's Champions of the World!

Tears filled the big Irish eyes of Tug McGraw as his teammates hugged and embraced him. Even though Tug had enjoyed a championship with the Mets in '69, he said the Phillies win was sweeter, because, "We had to come from behind in all but the final game!"

It would be about 3 a.m. before Tug and his teammates would finally leave Veterans Stadium. The celebration continued 'round the clock. Home-town parades would give every Philadelphia baseball fan an opportunity to thank the Phillies for this long-awaited championship.

Tug McGraw summed it up best: "There's no way we could have started off a new decade of baseball any better than this. I can't tell you how happy I am to be a part of this great American pastime."

Rose And Schmidt Rewrite Record Book

It's difficult to top a season like the Phils had in 1980, but no one could tell Pete Rose or Mike Schmidt that.

October 2, 1950 Robin Roberts notches his 20th victory of the season, defeating the mighty Brooklyn Dodgers to give Philadelphia its first N.L. Championship since 1915!

PHOTO
Charlie Hustle. Pete Rose rewrote the record books while playing for the Phils in the early 1980's.

Schmidt, the Phil's awesome home-run-hitter, came back in 1981 to win the National League's "Most Valuable Player" award for the second season in a row. He did it by leading the big leagues in homers for the fifth time in nine years. He was also N.L. leader in slugging percentage (.644), runs (78), walks (73), RBIs (91) and on-base percentage.

It was August 14, 1981, when Schmidt stepped into the batter's box to face Kent Tekulve, the Pittsburgh Pirates' side-arm relief ace. A moment later, Schmidt launched a missile deep into the second deck in right center to become the 44th player in major league history to hit over 300 homers. Five weeks later, Schmidt hit another boomer off Tekulve. This one — Schmidt's 310th career homer — broke the previous all-time Philadelphia record of 309 held by legendary Jimmie Foxx.

Yes, Schmidt was considered a hero by his fans, but he admitted to having his own hero to look up to.

"Pete Rose is my hero," said Schmidt. There is nobody playing baseball today in the big leagues, the minor leagues, Little League, anywhere that wouldn't like to play like Pete Rose."

Pete (nicknamed "Charlie Hustle") never quit giving 100 percent. He prided himself on always trying harder than any of his opponents. Pete Rose was all blisters, elbow grease and sweat. Even before coming to the Phils from the Cincinnati Reds in 1979, he had already assured a future place for himself in the Baseball Hall of Fame.

In Cincinatti, Pete had won three batting titles, the 1973 MVP, and the title, "Player of the Decade" for the 1970's. In 1978, Rose wound up his last year with the Reds by running off a 44-game hitting streak — a feat

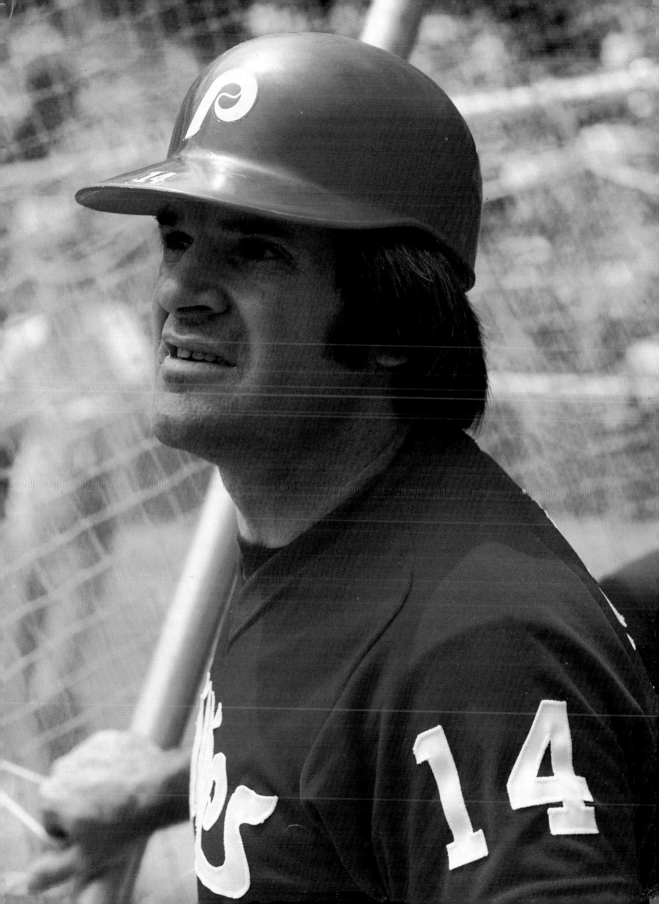

that had the entire nation mesmerized for weeks.

When he switched to the Phils in 1979, Rose was nearly 40, but he could still out-hustle any "kid" on the club.

"In 1980, it was Pete Rose who inspired this team to win the World Series," vowed Schmidt a year later.

In 1981, Pete played in every game, was second in the league in runs, led the league in hits and was second in the batting race. On August 10, he slashed a single off Mark Louis of the Cardinals to break Stan "The Man" Musial's all-time National League hits record of 3,631. On the all-time N.L. lists, he ranked first in at-bats, singles and hits.

But that was just the warm-up. In 1982, at the ripe old age of 41, Rose did such an outstanding job for the Phillies that it looked as if he might be pushing for "Player of the Decade" in the 1980's, too. Writing for the *Official Baseball Guide*, Hal Bodley chronicled a partial list of new milestones reached by Rose in '82:

• On June 22, Pete collected his 3,772nd hit, moving into second place on the all-time hits list ahead of Hank Aaron.

• On July 19, he collected his 3,800th hit.

• On August 14, his first at bat was his 12,365th, moving him into first place ahead of Aaron on the all-time list.

• On August 18, he had his 13,941st plate appearance, moving him into first place ahead of Aaron.

• On September 1, he made his 8,595th out, moving him into first place ahead of Aaron.

• On September 8, he played in his 3,077th game, also moving ahead of Aaron for first place on the National League all-time list.

1972
The great
Steve Carlton
pitches 15
consecutive
victories—a club
record that still
stands.

• He also played in his 626th consecutive game in 1982, becoming only the second player in baseball history to have two streaks of 500 consecutive games played.

• For the seventh time in his career, he compiled a hitting streak of 20 or more games, tying Ty Cobb for the most.

• At 41, he became only the fifth player in history to appear in 3,000 or more games.

The fans in Philadelphia felt fortunate. All through the 1981 and '82 seasons, they had a front-row seat for history-in-the-making, as Rose and Schmidt set record after record, week after week.

In 1981, the Phillies vied for the N.L. East Division championship, but were finally edged out by the Montreal Expos in the Division playoffs.

In 1982, they seized control of first place under new manager Pat Corrales and held on to the lead through most of the dog-days of late summer before finally slipping three games behind division champion St. Louis at the end. It was exciting baseball all the way. Southpaw Steve Carlton won the '82 Cy Young Award. Second baseman Manny Trillo — Mr. Perfect — set a major league record for most consecutive games without an error (89), and the Phils registered the best home record (51-30) of any National League Team!

Meanwhile, the Phillies had picked up new owners along the way. In October, 1981, Bill Giles had assembled a group of wealthy business people who purchased the club from the Carpenter Family for $30 million.

"I think this club is the bargain of the century at that price," said a smiling Bill Giles at the end of the 1982 campaign. He had just received news that the Phillies

PHOTO
The great one
in action. Here's
southpaw Steve
Carlton uncorking
one in the summer
of '82.

had drawn nearly 2.5 million fans to Veterans Stadium. It was the seventh straight season in which the Phils had finished a solid second in league attendance. Oh, those Philadelphia fans!

"Wheeze Kids" Lead Phils To Another N.L. Championship

While other teams in the league boasted new crops of rookie "whiz kids," the '83 Phillies featured an aging roster known as the gray-haired "Wheeze Kids." The combined ages of five starters — Pete Rose, Tony Perez, Steve Carlton, Ron Reed and Joe Morgan — added up to nearly 200 years. But age took a backseat to hustle with these guys, at least in the last half of the season.

Actually, the '83 Phillies had *two* seasons. From April through mid-July, they were the struggling, inconsistent team that played ho-hum .500 ball under Manager Pat Corrales.

On July 18, however, Paul Owens took over as manager and went on to transform the Phils into a rollicking powerhouse that swept through the N.L. on streak after streak through the end of the season. Owens' Phils were all but unbeatable in September, winning 22 of 29 games, including the major leagues' longest winning streak of the year — 11 games!

After clinching the division in September, the Phils easily toppled Tommy Lasorda's mighty L.A. Dodgers in the N.L. Championship Series.

Then it was on to the World Series against Joe Altobelli's deeply-experienced Baltimore Orioles. Now the Phils were facing the likes of Rick Dempsey, Eddie Murray, Ken Singleton, Scott McGregor, Mike Flana-

August 14, 1981 Mike Schmidt becomes the 44th player in major league history to hit 300 or more home runs.

PHOTO
In 1979, catcher Keith Moreland slammed the door on enemy runners at the plate.

PHOTO ABOVE
Phillies slugger
Mike Schmidt won
league MVP honors
two years in a
row (1980-81).

PHOTO ABOVE
Steve Carlton
showed come-from-
behind class in
this 1980 victory
over the K.C.
Royals.

gan and nine other veteran Orioles who had all played in the 1979 World Series against the Pittsburgh Pirates. Salty and seasoned, this Orioles club would refuse to wilt under the pressure of Philadelphia's vaunted hitting and pitching staffs.

It was a best-of-seven series, but the handwriting was already on the wall by Game 3. The Phils were counting on winning that contest by wheeling in their invincible weapon, Steve Carlton. As it turned out, Carlton did pitch brilliantly for six innings, but then he tired.

Owens probably should've sent in a reliever at that point. Instead, he left Carlton in. *Result*: With two out in the sixth, Baltimore's Rick Dempsey jumped on a lazy Carlton change-up, blasting a double into the left-center wall. Then Carlton threw a gopher ball, allowing Dempsey a free ride to third. Next, the Orioles' Benny Ayala tapped a single to left, scoring Dempsey. Carlton was yanked at that point, but the Orioles got one more run when right fielder, Dan Ford, hit a line drive past Philadelphia shortstop Ivan DeJesus scoring Ayala.

It was a demoralizing loss for the Phils, one from which they never really recovered. The Orioles went on to win the World Championship in five, but Owens and his "Wheeze Kids" could still hold their heads up high.

Give special credit . . . to Paul Owens who promised President Bill Giles a National League Championship—and delivered . . . to Steve Carlton who led the majors with 275 strikeouts in '83, posting his 300th career victory along the way . . . to Mike Schmidt who led the majors in homers for the sixth time in his career . . . and, of course, to Pete Rose for his attitude and inspiration.

For the first time in his long career, Rose had been

1982
Pete Rose becomes the fifth player in major league history to appear in 3,000 or more games.

PHOTO
The Phillies in the '80 Series. Del Unser clinches another win against Kansas City with this ninth-inning score.

benched during 1983. How did he take it? Owner Bill Giles explained, "I really believe the key to our winning the division after struggling most of the year was Pete Rose's attitude. The thing he did when he wasn't playing in September was not complain, and he rooted for the team. Gary Matthews said that made the team pull together."

At season's end, Pete was released by the Phils, much to the dismay of the Philadelphia fans. Instead of retiring, however, Rose signed on with his old club—the Reds—as player/manager. There, two years later, he finally broke one of the prestigious records in the game by passing Ty Cobb as baseball's all-time hit leader!

The "Master Rebuilders" Of The Mid-1980's

From 1984-86, the club did a Philadelphia shuffle. New faces appeared in the clubhouse as some players were traded or shuffled away, and new ones came in to take their place in the lineup. It was a confusing period for the fans. At times, it felt as if the "family" was being torn apart.

Veterans Pete Rose, Joe Morgan, Bob Dernier, Tony Perez, Ron Reed, Gary Matthews and Willie Hernandez were replaced for the 1984 season by newcomers such as John Wockenfuss, Jerry Koosman, Bill Campbell, Glenn Wilson and Mike Diaz.

"Let's experiment," said Manager Paul Owens, and he began to insert some of his young up-and-comers in the lineup. Two outfielders (Jeff Stone and John Russell), along with two infielders (Steve Jeltz and Rick Schu) all showed great promise for the future. Oh yes, rookie second baseman Juan Samuel stole 72 bases

and scored more than 100 runs. The Phils, however, finished a disappointing fourth in this, their first year of rebuilding.

More shuffling in 1985. John Felske took over as skipper. Catcher Bo Diaz was traded for a swift, hard-hitting shortstop by the name of Tom Foley. Mike Schmidt was moved from third to first. Young Juan Samuel continued to sparkle at second. A new crop of rookies, including Steve Keims (shortstop), John Russell (first base) and Jeff Stone (outfield) were given a shot. Despite a promising surge in August, however, Felske's Phillies eventually tumbled to fifth place, their lowest finish in 12 years.

"Have faith." That's what Phils' President Bill Giles told the fans. "This club is better than its record seems to show. Rebuilding takes time, but we're a year — maybe two — away from being a very good ball club."

Thrills Return To Veterans Stadium!

Giles was right. When the 1986 season rolled around, the Phillies were right back in the thick of things.

Sure, the mighty New York Mets won the division (and the World Series) that year, but the Phillies finished a strong second, while earning the distinction of being the only team in the league that had a winning record against the Mets!

By season's end, the press had nicknamed the Phils, "The Master Rebuilders," and for good reason. From May 28 on, the "new" Phillies had the third-best record in the entire National League, thanks to stellar play at nearly every position.

Pitching? Bruce Ruffin came out of nowhere to

1984
Juan Samuel sets a modern club record of 72 stolen bases. The following year, Samuel sets another club base-stealing mark by being caught 19 times!

PHOTO
Manny Trillo in one of his many picture-perfect double plays for the 1981 Phils.

45

1986
Ace reliever
Steve Bedrosian sets
an all-time Philly
record by pitching
29 saves.

become the best southpaw rookie pitcher in the majors. Shane Rawley was an All-Star. And Steve Bedrosian came out of the bullpen to slam the door for 29 saves, an all-time record for a Phillie reliever.

Infield? First baseman Von Hayes exploded for 19 homers, 186 hits, 98 RBIs and 24 thefts. Acrobatic second baseman Juan Samuel became the first player in N.L. history to reach double figures in doubles, triples, homers and stolen bases in each of his first three seasons. And the old war horse—38-year-old Mike Schmidt —led the league with 37 homers and 119 RBIs on the way to winning his 10th Gold Glove Award!

Outfield? Glenn Wilson led the league in assists for the second straight year, and Ron Roenicke came over from the Giants to get aboard in 60 of 69 games!

"I admit I'm a little surprised," said Schmidt with a grin at spring training, 1987. "I've been around this game a long time, and I thought I had seen everything. But to see a club rebuild as fast as we did . . . well, you just don't see it, that's all. I don't see any reason why we can't take it to the (World Champion) Mets this year."

As Schmidt and the rest of the Phillies took the field for the start of the 1987 campaign, *Sports Illustrated* magazine made the club its choice for "best everyday lineup in the league."

Yes, the spirit of Phillies legends such as Ed Delahanty, Jimmie Foxx, Casey Stengel, Grover Alexander, Robin Roberts and Dave Bancroft lives on in a new generation of Phils with names like Thompson, Hayes, Schmidt, Easler, Parrish, Wilson, Jeltz, Gross, Ruffin, Rawley, Carman, Tekulve and Bedrosian.

PHOTO
Kent Tekulve
sidearmed his
way to 11 victories
in 1986.